Leader Guide
FOR TWEENS

LEARNING TO STUDY THE BIBLE

L. J. Zimmerman

LEARNING TO STUDY THE BIBLE

PAGE 4
How to Use Learning to Study the Bible

PAGE 5
Bible Study Resources

PAGE 7
Preparing to Teach

PAGE 9
Session 1: Who? Author and Audience

PAGE 15
Session 2: What? Genre

PAGE 21
Session 3: When? Context

PAGE 27
Session 4: Where? Geography

PAGE 33
Session 5: Why? Interpretation

PAGE 39
Session 6: How? Read Closely

PAGE 45
Session 7: How? Reread

PAGE 51
Session 8: How? Read Together

Learning to Study the Bible
Leader Guide

Permission is granted to duplicate this page for local church use only. © 2018 Abingdon Press.

deepbluekids.com/learningtostudy

EDITORIAL / DESIGN TEAM

L. J. Zimmerman . . . . Editor
Theresa Kuhr. . . . . Production Editor
Arvis Guilbault . . . . Designer

ADMINISTRATIVE TEAM

Rev. Brian K. Milford . . . . President and Publisher
Marjorie M. Pon . . . Associate Publisher and Editor of Church School Publications (CSP)
Mary M. Mitchell . . . . Design Manager
Brittany Sky . . . . Senior Editor, Children's Resources

Written by: L. J. Zimmerman

Cover Design: Kellie Green; **Art:** Shutterstock®

LEARNING TO STUDY THE BIBLE: LEADER GUIDE. An official resource for The United Methodist Church approved by Discipleship Ministries and published by Abingdon Press, a division of The United Methodist Publishing House, 2222 Rosa L. Parks Blvd., PO Box 280988, Nashville, TN 37228-0988. Price: $14.99. Copyright © 2018 Abingdon Press. All rights reserved. Printed in the United States of America.

For information concerning permission to reproduce any material in this publication, write to Rights and Permissions, The United Methodist Publishing House, 2222 Rosa L. Parks Blvd., PO Box 280988, Nashville, TN 37228-0988. You may fax your request to 615-749-6128. Or e-mail permissions@umpublishing.org.

If you have questions or comments, call toll free: 800-672-1789. Or e-mail customerhelp@cokesbury.com.

To order copies of this publication, call toll free: **800-672-1789**. You may fax your order to 800-445-8189. Telecommunication Device for the Deaf/Telex Telephone: 800-227-4091. Or order online at **cokesbury.com**. Use your Cokesbury account, American Express, Visa, Discover, or MasterCard.

Scripture quotations are taken from the Common English Bible. Copyright © 2011 by the Common English Bible. All rights reserved. Used by permission.

18 19 20 21 22 23 24 25 26 27—10 9 8 7 6 5 4 3 2 1

ISBN: 9781501856280
PACP10526752-01

How to Use Learning to Study the Bible

By fifth and sixth grade, kids are typically capable of reading, writing, and discussing what they've read. At this age, it's time to dive deeper into the biblical text by exploring its history and methods of interpretation. **Learning to Study the Bible** gives students the tools they need to explore the Bible using the classic questions: Who? What? When? Where? Why? and How?

The primary component of **Learning to Study the Bible** is the Student Journal. Leaders guide students in conducting their own Bible studies using their Student Journal. The leader's role is to introduce ideas, ask questions, and keep the students on track.

You will lead a group of tweens through the Student Journal over the course of eight sessions. Sessions are meant to last about forty-five minutes or an hour. Each session has four parts: Explore, Study, Reflect, and Share.

1. **Explore:** Students play a group game to warm up, and read a short introduction to the session's topic from their Student Journals. Then they try it out, completing a short activity in small groups or pairs.

2. **Study:** Students take the concept they've explored and apply it to the Bible. They study a Bible story or passage together, and use the appropriate Bible study resources (see pages 5-6) to investigate further.

3. **Reflect:** After studying the text, the students reflect individually using a journaling prompt, and then reflect as a group.

4. **Share:** The students brainstorm ways to share what they've learned with their community. It will be your responsibility as a Leader to give the students opportunities to share their newfound knowledge and skills. Check out the Share section of each lesson in advance and make arrangements for your students to present their findings to the appropriate group.

Studying the Bible with tweens is an exciting and sometimes daunting adventure. Remember, the journey of Bible study is lifelong. You don't need to have all the answers! You just need to be open to investigating this sacred text with your tweens. Use the Preparing to Teach reflection on page 7 to ready yourself for this holy work.

Learning to Study the Bible Resources

Items needed for this study are:

Class Pack (PDF Download)
ISBN: 9781501856303

Student Journal (one per student)
ISBN: 9781501856273

Leader Guide (one per Leader; available in two formats)

ebook: ISBN: 9781501856297
Print: ISBN: 9781501856280

Bible Study Resources

As you embark on this Bible study journey with your tweens, you'll soon discover that there is a plethora of Bible study helps out there to choose from. It can be confusing to navigate through the multitude of commentaries, dictionaries, concordances, handbooks, atlases, and other biblical companion pieces.

Each lesson in this study instructs students to use certain types of Bible study tools to investigate a text. It can be tempting to search online for free versions of these resources. However, the resources that are readily available online are not always compatible with the assumptions of this study (see page 7). Not every free commentary, for example, uses historical criticism to study the Bible. Not every Bible handbook encourages readers to ask questions and to look at the text from multiple angles.

Because we know it is difficult to find and access helpful Bible study tools, we have created a website where you can access the relevant pages of our CEB Bible study resources for most lessons.

Simply visit **deepbluekids.com/learningtostudy** and download the file corresponding to the session number. Each file contains content relevant to that session from the *CEB Study Bible, CEB Student Bible, CEB Bible Dictionary, CEB Concordance,* and the *Abingdon New Interpreter's Bible Commentary.* This download is FREE.

Another useful, free resource is your local public library. Many libraries carry Bible study resources, including commentaries, handbooks, dictionaries, and so forth. Following is a list of recommended resources to use in conjunction with this study.

Common English Bible Resources

We believe that the Common English Bible (CEB) is the most responsibly translated, easy-to-read English version of the Bible. We recommend using the CEB translation whenever reading the Bible with your students, as well as the additional CEB resources that can be accessed on our website. The CEB Bible study resources are listed below.

- *The CEB Study Bible*. Edited by Joel B. Green. Nashville: Common English Bible, 2011.
- *The CEB Student Bible*. Edited by Elizabeth Corrie. Nashville: Common English Bible, 2015.
- *The Deep Blue Kids Bible*. Nashville: Common English Bible, 2012.
- *The CEB Women's Bible*. Edited by Jaime Clark-Soles. Nashville: Common English Bible, 2016.
- *Bible Dictionary: The Common English Bible*. Nashville: Common English Bible, 2011.
- *The Deep Blue Kids Bible Dictionary*. Edited by Laura Allison. Nashville: Abingdon Press, 2017.
- *Concise Concordance: The Common English Bible*. Nashville: Common English Bible, 2011.

Free Bible Study Resources

Scan this code to download FREE sample pages from the *CEB Study Bible, CEB Student Bible, CEB Bible Dictionary, CEB Concordance,* and the *Abingdon New Interpreter's Bible Commentary.* You'll find all the relevant pages for each session, so your tweens can study the Bible with the help of trustworthy scholarship, for free! (If you don't have a QR code reader, type **deepbluekids.com/learningtostudy** into your browser.)

Recommended Commentaries

- *The New Interpreter's Bible One-Volume Commentary.* Edited by Beverly Roberts Gaventa and David Petersen. Nashville: Abingdon Press, 2010.
- *The Women's Bible Commentary.* Edited by Carol A. Newsom, Sharon H. Ringe, and Jacqueline E. Lapsley. 3rd ed. Louisville: Westminster John Knox Press, 2012.
- *HarperCollins Bible Commentary.* Edited by James L. Mays, et al.; Rev. ed. San Francisco: HarperCollins, 2000.
- *The Oxford Bible Commentary.* Edited by John Barton and John Muddiman. Oxford: Oxford University Press, 2001.
- *The IVP Bible Background Commentary: Old Testament.* Edited by John H. Walton, Victor H. Matthews, and Mark W. Chavalas. Downers Grove, IL: InterVarsity Press, 2000.
- *The IVP Bible Background Commentary: New Testament.* Edited by Craig S. Keener. Downers Grove, IL: InterVarsity Press, 2014.

Recommended Bible Handbooks

- *The Essential Bible Handbook.* Nashville: Abingdon Press, 2009.
- *The Complete Bible Handbook: An Illustrated Companion,* by John Bowker. New York: DK Publishing, 2001.
- *The Eerdmans Companion to the Bible.* Edited by Gordon D. Fee and Robert L. Hubbard, Jr., Grand Rapids: Wm. B. Eerdmans Publishing Co., 2011.
- *The Oxford Companion to the Bible.* Edited by Bruce M. Metzger and Michael D. Coogan. Oxford: Oxford University Press, 2004.

Recommended Bible Dictionaries (Non-CEB)

- *HarperCollins Bible Dictionary.* Edited by Mark Allan Powell. Revised and updated. 3rd ed. New York: HarperOne, The Society of Biblical Literature, 2011.
- *Eerdmans Dictionary of the Bible.* Edited by David Noel Freedman. Grand Rapids: Wm. B. Eerdmans Publishing Co., 2000.

Preparing to Teach

Most Sunday school classes for children aim to teach the content of Bible stories. They build a foundation for children's faith by giving them the basic outline of the stories of the Bible. As kids get older, they come to Sunday school less and less. Whether or not they return to Sunday school or Bible study as adults, it's important that they have the tools to read and interpret the Bible for themselves.

The goal of **Learning to Study the Bible** is to equip students to read and study the Bible for themselves. Students need more than simply a lesson with a Bible concordance or commentary. They need someone to guide them in exploring the basic questions of interpretation: what is the Bible, and what does it mean to me?

This curriculum is written with several assumptions about the Bible:

- The Bible is a living text. While it was written hundreds or thousands of years ago, it continues to speak to people of faith today, and is interpreted in a variety of contexts and cultures.
- The Bible was created in a historical context very different from our own. Learning about the historical context of the Bible and its authors enriches our understanding of the text.
- Biblical interpretation is an act of faith, guided by the Holy Spirit.
- Every reader has interpretive lenses, ways of seeing the world that affect his or her interpretation of the text.
- There are many interpretive layers between ourselves and the biblical text, in the form of translators, scribes, copyists, editors, authors, and oral storytellers.

Take a moment to consider what you think about these assumptions. Which of them strike you? What assumptions about the Bible do you bring to this study?

The Bible is an important book in Western culture. References to the Bible abound in books, movies, and popular culture. There are many different teachings, both explicit and implicit, about what the Bible is and why it matters to our lives. Some of those teachings have been damaging to people of faith. What were you taught about the Bible growing up? Did you find your education about the Bible helpful? Why or why not?

Differing interpretations of the Bible have fueled many bitter fights among Christians over the centuries. Even the formation of the biblical canon caused a stir! Tweens are not ignorant of religious controversy in the world. What are some controversial topics that come up for you when you think about studying the Bible? What topics do you think your tweens might have questions about? How can you respond in a loving, encouraging way?

Take some time to pray for the students in your Bible study. If you know who will be participating, list their names here. Doodle or draw around their names as you lift them up to God. Remember that God is big enough to handle all our questions, all our doubts, and all our wrestling with the Bible.

Who? Author and Audience

Why does this matter?

Some Bibles for sale on *amazon.com* list their author as "God." This reference to the divine inspiration of the sacred Scriptures is amusing, but it clouds an important reality. God's word comes to us through real people. The people who created the Scriptures as we know them were humans like us: people who told the stories of their faith, wrote them down, edited them, compiled them, and painstakingly copied them over the centuries. The people who created the Bible were deeply invested in their own faith, and in passing on their traditions to others.

What we find in the Bible is the embodied Word of God—embodied by those who originally spoke and wrote the words. God's truth comes to us in human-shaped containers. The humans bearing God's word spoke certain languages, had particular beliefs about the world, and had relationships with their original audiences. Much of that information is lost to us. But what we can discover about the authors of the Scriptures enriches our understanding of the words.

Sometimes the Bible itself tells us about its authors. Psalm 51 is attributed to King David, for example. This psalm of contrition is much more meaningful because we can read up on the back-story (2 Samuel 11-12). Paul's letter to the Philippians is made richer by knowing the story of Paul founding the Philippian church with Lydia (Acts 16:11-40).

In other instances, our ability to get to know the author is guesswork based on the text itself. The Book of Isaiah, for example, is suspected to be composed by three different individuals, then compiled into one prophetic book. Biblical scholars identify these three "Isaiahs" by their writing style, the historical references they include, and the themes they take up. Knowing that the original Isaiah wrote from a crumbling Israelite kingdom, while a later "ghost writer" wrote from the Babylonian exile, gives the text new shades of meaning.

Knowledge of the people who wrote and received the Bible isn't essential to interpretation. God's word continues to speak in new contexts. But connecting, even in a small way, with the humans on the other side of the stories might bring them to life in a new way for your students.

Supplies

- Bibles (CEB)
- Bible dictionary (CEB)
- Student Journals
- sticky notes
- pens, colored pencils, markers
- dry-erase board and marker set
- presentation supplies such as posterboard, video camera, computer/tablet
- unused tube of lip balm

Learning Goals

- Spark curiosity about the authors and original audiences of the Bible
- Introduce and use a Bible dictionary
- Sharpen deductive reasoning skills in biblical interpretation

In the Brain of a Tween

You may think you need to have all the answers in order to do an in-depth Bible study for tweens. I've got good news for you: you don't! In fact, your students will probably prefer it if you avoid handing them answers. Instead, let the students take the lead in the investigation. Your job is to ask good questions, encourage their imagination, and intervene as needed to keep the group on track.

Tweens are naturally very curious, but they may not feel comfortable training their curiosity on the Bible. If they've been discouraged from questioning in the past, or taught that there is only one correct interpretation of a given Bible story, they may feel afraid to explore.

Remind the students that you're with them on the journey—even adults have questions and want to learn more! Bring your own questions about Bible people and be sure to remind the students that it's okay not to have all the answers.

Explore

PLAY TOGETHER—GUESS WHO?

○ Before class, make a sticky note with the name of a famous person for each student. Suggested names include: George Washington, Elvis Presley, Albert Einstein, Queen Elizabeth, Walt Disney, J. K. Rowling, Martin Luther King Jr., and so forth.

○ As students arrive, stick a sticky note to their backs. Begin class by inviting students to mingle with one another, asking yes-or-no questions to ascertain their identities.

○ **ASK:** What information helped you discover which famous person you were?

○ **SAY:** Now we're going to play a different kind of "guess who" game. We're going to see what information we can discover about the people who wrote the Bible.

EXPLORE THE THEME

○ Invite students to take turns reading pages 2-3 of their Student Journals out loud.

○ **ASK:** What questions do you have about the people who created the Bible?

○ Write the students' questions on the dry-erase board. As you continue the session, revisit the questions to see how many you were able to answer about the apostle Paul.

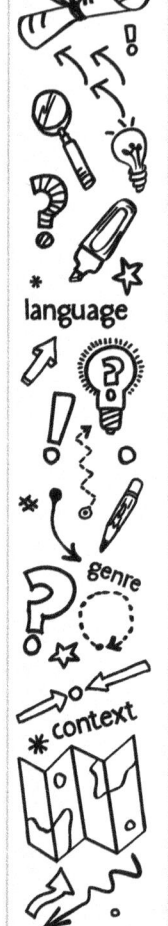

Who Wrote the Bible?

Well, that's an interesting question.

Let's start with the basics. **The Bible isn't just one book.** It's actually a collection of books—like a library. Sixty-six books, to be exact.

Does that mean there were sixty-six authors of the Bible? Not exactly.

Some books are collections of stories that used to be passed down orally. Before they were written down, people told the stories around fires, at meals, and before bed. The stories were well-known, and everyone told them in a slightly different way. It would be nearly impossible to identify the true "author" of these stories. Instead, we call the person who wrote all the stories down the "editor."

Another thing that makes it hard to tell exactly how many people wrote the Bible is pseudonyms. Pseudonyms are false names. People might use the name of a more famous person to give their writing an extra boost in popularity. One example is in the Book of Ecclesiastes. The author claims to be a king of Israel, implying King Solomon, who was known for his wisdom. But evidence suggests that the book was probably written hundreds of years after King Solomon lived.

2

EXPLORE

○ Play Together—Guess Who?
○ Explore the Theme
○ Try It Out—Behind the Texts

STUDY

○ Connect It—Bible Person Profile
○ Read a Text—Second Timothy
○ Use a Tool—Bible Dictionary

10 Learning to Study the Bible
Leader Guide: Session 1

Permission is granted to duplicate this page for local church use only. © 2018 Abingdon Press.

deepbluekids.com/learningtostudy

Behind the Texts

Here are some text conversations recovered from a random individual's phone. What can you tell me about this person, just based on their text conversations?

TRY IT OUT—BEHIND THE TEXTS

○ Invite students to pair up and complete the Behind the Texts activity on pages 4-5 of their Student Journals.

○ Invite each pair of students to share their responses.

○ **ASK:** Were you surprised by how much you could learn about the people who wrote these texts? Why or why not?

REFLECT

○ Journal
○ Discuss
○ So, What?

SHARE

○ Make a Plan
○ Get to Work
○ Blessing

Learning to Study the Bible
Leader Guide: Session 1

Study

CONNECT IT—BIBLE PERSON PROFILE

○ Invite the students to turn to pages 6-7 of their Student Journals. Have them divide the Scripture passages among themselves and look them up in small groups or pairs, then use the information they discover to create a social media profile for Paul.

○ **ASK:** What do we know about Paul based on these passages?

○ Invite students to write their responses on the dry-erase board to create Paul's "profile." They may choose to mimic the social media profile template in the Student Journal.

READ A TEXT—SECOND TIMOTHY

○ Have the students find 2 Timothy 1:3-14 in their Bibles and take turns reading the passage aloud, each student reading a sentence.

○ **ASK:** How does the information you learned about Paul affect how you read this passage? Who is Paul writing to? What can you tell about Timothy from this passage?

USE A TOOL

○ Invite the students to look up Paul/Saul and Timothy in a Bible dictionary.

○ **ASK:** What did you learn about Paul? about Timothy?

○ **SAY:** Bible dictionaries compile important information about Bible people, so you don't have to read every verse about them to make a profile.

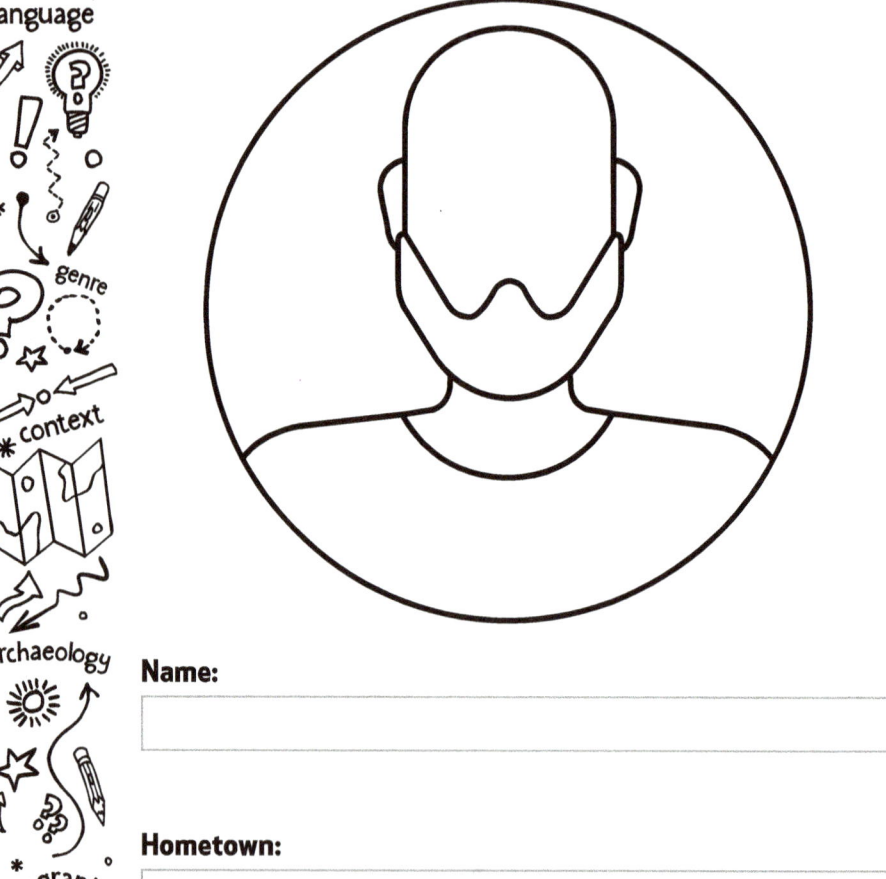

12 Learning to Study the Bible Leader Guide: Session 1

Permission is granted to duplicate this page for local church use only. © 2018 Abingdon Press.

deepbluekids.com/learningtostudy

Journal

Does learning about the people who wrote the Bible change how you see the Scriptures? Why or why not?

8

Reflect

JOURNAL
- Invite the students to spend some time in individual reflection, responding to the prompt on page 8 of their Student Journals.

DISCUSS
- Invite the students to share their responses as they feel comfortable.
- **ASK:** Do you think Paul realized that his letters would become sacred Scripture? Do you think he would have written any differently if he had?

SO, WHAT?
- **ASK:** Why does it matter if you know about the people who wrote the Bible? What difference does it make? How would you summarize our discussion today in one sentence?

Share

MAKE A PLAN

- **SAY:** Your challenge this week is to find a way to share what you've learned about the apostle Paul with your family. You can do that in whatever way you like. You can create a video, a skit, a poster, a computer presentation, or plan an activity to do together. You can work together or in pairs to make your plan.

GET TO WORK

- After the students have decided how they want to share Paul's profile, they can use the remaining time together to execute their plan. Make presentation supplies such as posterboard, video cameras, and a computer available for their use.

BLESSING

- Invite your students to bless each other as they prepare to go out and share what they've learned. Students may anoint one another's hands with an unused tube of lip balm while saying a simple blessing, such as "God be with you as you share the good news." Save the lip balm to use throughout this study. Use it each week for this Blessing activity.

Notes

What? Genre

Why does this matter?

In the 1999 movie *Galaxy Quest*, the washed-up stars of a popular 1970s science fiction show are visited by aliens. The aliens beam the actors onto their spaceship and explain that they've discovered their "historical documents" and have proudly modeled their society after them. What they've really discovered are reruns of the science fiction show. They've made a mistake in genre.

It's an easy mistake to make. The television show is a broadcast from another society, in another time and place. But as this light-hearted comedy illustrates, making a mistake in genre can skew one's entire interpretation. Modern readers of the Bible face a similar challenge as the aliens in *Galaxy Quest*. We have stories and writings that have come to us from another society, in another time and place. One of the first major questions we face when trying to interpret these texts is that of genre.

Genre is the category in which a piece of literature belongs. Some examples of biblical genres include: poetry, worship songs, historical records, parables, narratives, satire, letters, and apocalyptic literature. Each genre has its own forms and style by which it is identified. Biblical poetry often uses parallelism, hyperbole, and metaphors. Letters often identify the author and audience in the first lines. Historical records list kings and events.

Some genres are easier to identify than others. Satire, for example, is often tricky. Think of how many people post articles from satirical news websites without realizing they aren't true—and those are articles from our own time and place! Bible readers have even more difficulty identifying certain genres because of our lack of familiarity with the social and literary conventions of biblical societies.

Because of those barriers, we often must rely on biblical scholars who have researched other ancient writings to help us identify genre. You and your students don't have to become experts in the forms of biblical case law to understand the ten commandments. The important thing is to simply recognize that genre matters and know how to investigate biblical genres.

Supplies

- study Bibles (CEB, KJV)
- Bible dictionary (CEB)
- Bible commentary
- Student Journals
- Class Pack
- dry-erase board and marker set
- pens, colored pencils, markers
- scissors
- presentation supplies such as posterboard, video camera, computer/tablet

Learning Goals

- Introduce and explore biblical genres
- Learn to use Bible commentaries and study Bibles to identify possible genres of texts
- Explore the significance of genre for biblical interpretation

In the Brain of a Tween

You may think you need to have all the answers in order to do an in-depth Bible study for tweens. I've got good news for you: you don't! In fact, your students will probably prefer it if you avoid handing them answers. Instead, let the students take the lead in the investigation. Your job is to ask good questions, encourage their imagination, and intervene as needed to keep the group on track.

Tweens are likely to only hear the word *genre* in English class. They may not have made the connection between interpreting classic novels and interpreting other texts—from the Bible to the ads that pop up as they browse the web. Everything has a genre. Tweens may have been taught that the Bible is one book with only one genre. Remind the students that the Bible is full of many different kinds of writings, and God speaks to us in many ways! Remind your tweens that it's amazing to have these ancient writings passed down to us, and it's our job to read them carefully and try to interpret them as best we can.

Explore

PLAY TOGETHER—MATCH IT UP

○ Before class, print the Match It Up Cards (Class Pack—p. 1) and cut them out.

○ Mix up the cards and lay them facedown in a grid on the table. Invite students to take turns flipping two cards. If the cards match, the student may keep the pair and flip another two cards. If they don't match, the student flips the cards back over and the next student takes a turn.

○ Green cards have the name of a genre, or category of writing, while red cards have an opening line. Students must figure out which genre matches each opening line to form a pair. Students may mistake the genre of a line. Keep track so you can verify whether students have found a match.

○ **ASK:** How did you identify what genre each line belonged to?

○ **SAY:** Genres are categories of writing. There are always clues in the text to let you know what its genre is. Some clues are more obvious than others.

EXPLORE THE THEME

○ Invite students to take turns reading pages 10-11 of their Student Journals out loud.

○ **ASK:** What kinds of genres do you think are included in the Bible?

What Is the Bible, Anyway?

What kind of book is the Bible? Or, more accurately, what kinds of *books* are in the Bible? (Remember when we talked about how the Bible is really a collection of 66 books?!) What section of a bookstore or a library do you think you would find each book of the Bible in, if they were separated?

These questions are all about **genre**, or the category a piece of writing belongs to. The books of the Bible come from many different genres—poetry, narrative, history, personal letters, and more. We can tell a book's genre by reading it carefully and looking for clues. Just like today we know a story that starts out "Once upon a time …" is a fairy tale, in biblical times,

10

EXPLORE
○ Play Together—Match It Up
○ Explore the Theme
○ Try It Out—Category Clues

STUDY
○ Connect It—Translating Genre
○ Read a Text—Jonah
○ Use Some Tools—Study Bible, Bible Dictionary, Commentary

Category Clues

Discovering the genre of a text is a bit like being a detective—it's all about clues. Let's make a list of clues to identify different genres, or categories of writing.

List all the ways you can tell if something is:

- *a poem*
- *a letter*
- a sermon

TRY IT OUT—CATEGORY CLUES

○ Invite students to pair up and complete the Category Clues activity on pages 12-13 of their Student Journals.

○ Invite each pair of students to share their responses.

○ **ASK:** Do you think you can use these same clues to tell what genre a book of the Bible belongs to? Why or why not?

REFLECT

○ Journal
○ Discuss
○ So, What?

SHARE

○ Make a Plan
○ Get to Work
○ Blessing

Learning to Study the Bible
Leader Guide: Session 2

Study

CONNECT IT—TRANSLATING GENRE

○ **SAY:** In the original Hebrew text of the Old Testament, there were no vowels, punctuation, verse numbers, or formatting. All of that is added for you by the people who copied and translated the Bible. They had to decide when each sentence and section ended and began, and how to format the text depending on what genre they thought it was.

○ Invite the students to read page 14 of their Student Journals, and to look up Jonah 2 in two translations of the Bible (CEB and KJV).

○ **ASK:** What genre does each translator assign to the passage? How can you tell?

○ Invite the students to try their hand at choosing punctuation and formatting for a biblical text by completing the activity on page 15 of their Student Journals. Afterwards, invite the students to share and compare their responses *before looking up* the passage in a Bible.

READ A TEXT—JONAH

○ If you have time, have the students take turns reading the entire Book of Jonah. Otherwise, invite the students to read an abridged version: 1:1-6, 11-12, 15 and 17; 2:1 and 10; 3:3-5 and 10; 4:1-11.

○ **ASK:** What genre do you think the Book of Jonah is? What clues are in the story to let you know?

Translating Genre

Did you know that the original Hebrew text of the Old Testament didn't have vowels, capitalization, punctuation, verse numbers, or formatting? Check it out:

Vowels and paragraph divisions were added to the Hebrew text between the sixth and tenth centuries—hundreds of years after the original texts were written. The chapter and verse numbers we use today were added in the twelfth century. All the rest of the punctuation—indents, question marks, quotation marks, and everything else—is up to modern translators to decide.

These details are important because vocabulary, punctuation, and formatting are major clues to genre. Check out Jonah,

USE SOME TOOLS

○ Invite the students to look up the Book of Jonah in a study Bible and Bible commentary. Typically, possible genres are discussed in the introduction to a book. Have the students look Jonah up in a Bible dictionary as well, along with any unfamiliar terms.

○ **ASK:** What genres do the commentators assign to Jonah? How would your interpretation of

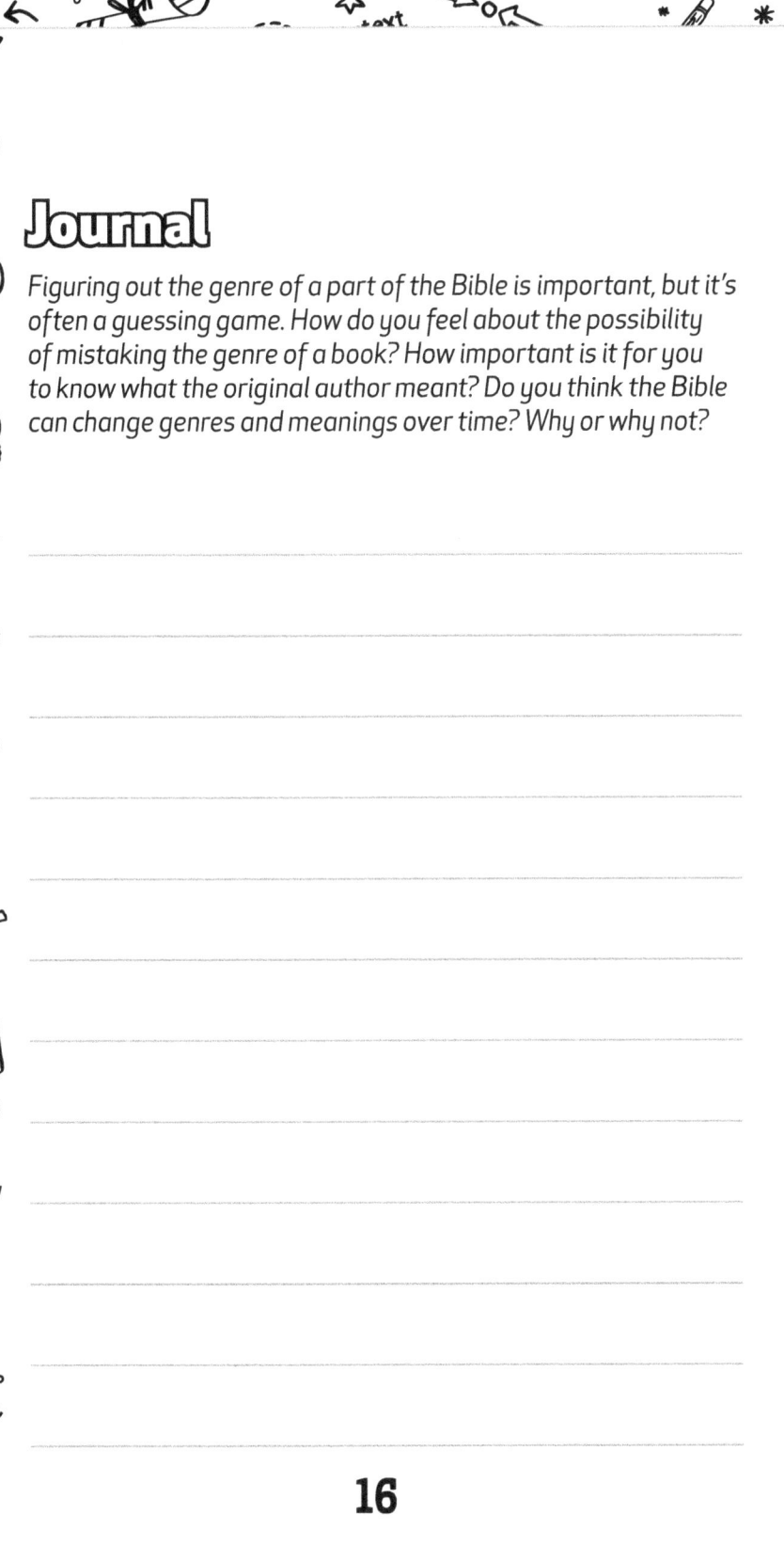

Reflect

JOURNAL
○ Invite the students to spend some time in individual reflection, responding to the prompt on page 16 of their Student Journals.

DISCUSS
○ Invite the students to share their responses as they feel comfortable.
○ **ASK:** Do you believe God still speaks through the Bible, even if the original meaning is lost to us? Why or why not?

SO, WHAT?
○ **ASK:** Why does genre matter when you're interpreting the Bible? What difference does it make? How would you summarize our discussion today in one sentence?

the story be different depending on the genre you assume?

○ **SAY:** Study Bibles and Bible commentaries are written by scholars who study the Bible in its historical context. But remember that commentators are just people, sharing their best interpretations with us. You bring your own insights and questions to the Bible. It's okay to disagree with a commentary.

Share

MAKE A PLAN

- Before class, identify an adult Sunday school class or small group that would appreciate learning from your students.
- **SAY:** Your challenge this week is to find a way to share what you've learned about genre and the Book of Jonah with the adults in our church. You can do that in whatever way you like. You can create a video, a skit, a poster, a computer presentation, or plan an activity to do together. You need to work as a group to make your plan.

GET TO WORK

- After the students have decided how they want to share their findings, they can use the remaining time together to execute their plan. Make appropriate materials such as posterboard, video cameras, and a computer available for their use. If possible, have the students present to their adult pupils during the last ten to fifteen minutes of your time together. If not, schedule another time to present.

BLESSING

- Invite your students to bless each other as they prepare to go out and share what they've learned. Students may anoint one another's hands with an unused tube of lip balm while saying a simple blessing, such as "God be with you as you share the good news."

Notes

When? Context

Why does this matter?

When children are in grade school, their reading skills improve and they begin to encounter new vocabulary. They're taught to work out the meaning of unfamiliar words by using "context clues." Many adults still do this reflexively, because they know that words can take on different meanings depending on the context. *Gross* can mean "yucky" when your child says it, but it typically means "the overall total" when it's printed on your paycheck.

The meaning of any given word is dependent on the words around it, because languages are systems. And languages are produced by societies, which are systems of people. The meanings of words, phrases, and whole stories change as society changes. Take the word *nice*. In the fourteenth century, *nice* meant "ignorant" or "foolish." Over hundreds of years, the word has changed meanings several times, landing on "agreeable." An insult has become a compliment.

When modern readers encounter a biblical text, contexts collide. It's easy to forget that the Bible was created in another language and society when we're reading it on our phones. Most modern readers bring their own linguistic and cultural understandings to bear on the Bible without even realizing that they are doing so. People only tend to remember the contextual divide between themselves and the text when the stories are so strange and archaic, they can't seamlessly absorb them into their modern worldview.

The truth is, context always matters in interpretation, whether or not the reader is aware of it. Anytime one of your students picks up the Bible, there are at least three contexts to consider—the literary context, the historical context, and the cultural context of your student. The students are already familiar with their own cultural context. How do they become familiar with the literary and historical contexts of the Bible?

They become archaeologists, detectives, and metaphorical time travelers. Historians, biblical archaeologists, linguists, and other scholars have done the research. Bible dictionaries, commentaries, and handbooks contain condensed versions of that research. Using these tools, students can discover the biblical "context clues" that shed new light on texts.

Supplies

- study Bibles (CEB)
- Bible dictionary (CEB)
- Bible commentary
- Bible handbook
- Student Journals
- Class Pack
- dry-erase board and marker set
- pens, colored pencils, markers
- scissors
- presentation supplies such as posterboard, video camera, computer/tablet

Learning Goals

- Investigate the connection between context and meaning
- Spark curiosity about biblical and modern cultural contexts
- Use Bible dictionaries, commentaries, and handbooks to research biblical context

In the Brain of a Tween

You may think you need to have all the answers in order to do an in-depth Bible study for tweens. I've got good news for you: you don't! In fact, your students will probably prefer it if you avoid handing them answers. Instead, let the students take the lead in the investigation. Your job is to ask good questions, encourage their imagination, and intervene as needed to keep the group on track.

Some tweens will have had the benefit of cross-cultural experiences in their life, but many tweens have only considered the world from their own cultural perspective. Cultural assumptions are usually taken for granted until another culture is encountered. The Bible brings another culture into the room, and is ripe for cross-cultural encounter if we allow it to unfold. Help your tweens develop a healthy curiosity about life in biblical times and the meaning of the stories to their original audiences.

Explore

PLAY TOGETHER—CONTEXT CLUES

○ Before class, print the Context Clues Cards (Class Pack—p. 2) and cut them out.

○ One at a time, go through the cards with the students. Invite the students to try to identify what they are looking at in each picture. (Each card is a real photograph. Cover the answer in the bottom corner with your finger.)

○ **ASK:** Which card was the easiest to identify? Which was the hardest? Why?

○ **SAY:** When you're trying to identify something, it helps to see its context—what's around it. It's the same with words, ideas, and stories. When we interpret the Bible, understanding context is very important.

EXPLORE THE THEME

○ Invite students to take turns reading pages 18-19 of their Student Journals out loud.

○ **ASK:** What do you think a person from Bible times would say if they time traveled to our world? What might surprise them or impress them?

Contextualize It

context (noun) \kän-tekst\ | the group of conditions that exist where and when something happens. From the Latin *contextere*, "to weave together."

What's up? What's down? What's going on around you? Are you a fish swimming in a pond? Are you a bird flying in the air? Are you a snail sliding along the ground, oozing a trail of goo? Whatever is happening in your world, whatever circumstances affect your everyday life, that's your "historical context."

In most American cities, our context includes things like

- the fact that you can take a car or bus to school;
- the ability to instantly get in touch with people hundreds of miles away through e-mail and phones;
- the fact that most kids in your community—both boys and girls—learn how to read; and
- the ability to buy fresh fruits and vegetables from the grocery store all year round.

18

EXPLORE

○ Play Together—Context Clues

○ Explore the Theme

○ Try It Out—Alien Archaeologist

STUDY

○ Connect It—Before and After

○ Read a (Con)Text—Luke 6:1-11

○ Use Some Tools—Study Bible, Bible Dictionary, Commentary, Bible Handbook

Alien Archaeologist

Imagine you're an alien from a distant planet. You've just completed your first successful space travel mission and landed on Earth. You begin exploring and encounter the following objects/items. Write what you think each item might be for. Remember, you know absolutely NOTHING about human culture.

hair straightener

carousel

20

TRY IT OUT—ALIEN ARCHAEOLOGIST

○ Invite students to pair up and complete the Alien Archaeologist activity on pages 20-21 of their Student Journals.

○ Invite each pair of students to share their responses.

○ **ASK:** What other objects might be confusing to an alien archaeologist? How is the Alien Archaeologist game similar to the research of biblical archaeologists?

REFLECT
○ Journal
○ Discuss
○ So, What?

SHARE
○ Make a Plan
○ Get to Work
○ Blessing

Learning to Study the Bible
Leader Guide: Session 3

Permission is granted to duplicate this page for local church use only. © 2018 Abingdon Press.

deepbluekids.com/learningtostudy **23**

Study

CONNECT IT—BEFORE AND AFTER

- Invite the students to turn to pages 22-23 of their Student Journals. Have them look up Luke 6:1-11 in their Bibles and read the story out loud.

- Divide the students into two groups. Have one group read the section before (Luke 5:33-39) and one group read the section after the passage (Luke 6:12-19). Have each group record their observations in their Student Journal on page 23 in the appropriate column.

- **ASK:** How is this passage connected to what comes before it? To what comes after it? Does knowing what comes before and after the story affect your interpretation? Why or why not?

READ A (CON)TEXT—LUKE 6:1-11

- **SAY:** Now that we've looked into the literary context of this passage, it's time to investigate the historical context.

- **ASK:** What questions do you have about the context of this passage that you'd like to investigate?

- Write the students' questions on a dry-erase board. If the students need help, offer suggestions: Who were the Pharisees and legal experts? What law was Jesus breaking? What is the story about David? What's a withered hand? Why were the Pharisees mad about Jesus healing someone?

Before and After

Whenever you study a Bible passage—in church, Sunday school, Bible study, or on your own—it's important to do a before-and-after check. That means reading a few verses before the section and a few verses after the section to see if there's any important information that can help you understand the passage.

Another option is to look up the introduction to the book you're reading in a study Bible or commentary. Most of the time, Bible scholars make an outline of the book, meaning they break it up into sections based on major themes. Check and see what section your passage is in. What's it called? How does it fit into the book as a whole?

Let's try it out. Look up Luke 6:1-11. Write down what you think the main points of the passage are here:

○ _____

○ _____

○ _____

○ _____

22

USE SOME TOOLS

- Divide the students into small groups and invite them to investigate their questions using the study Bibles, commentary, Bible dictionary, and Bible handbook.

- **ASK:** What information have you gathered? How does this information shed light on our story?

- **SAY:** We have many tools available to help us investigate

Journal

Do you think the Bible can still be meaningful to your daily life when you live in such a different historical context? Why or why not?

Reflect

JOURNAL
- Invite the students to spend some time in individual reflection, responding to the prompt on page 24 of their Student Journals.

DISCUSS
- Invite the students to share their responses as they feel comfortable.
- **ASK:** What do you think are the major cultural differences between our time and biblical times?

SO, WHAT?
- **ASK:** Why does the historical context of the Bible matter? What difference does it make? How would you summarize our discussion today in one sentence?

our questions about the Bible. But even with all this research, there will still be some things we can't find answers for. That's okay. God still speaks to us through the Bible, even though we live in a very different context from the original authors.

Share

MAKE A PLAN

- Before class, check in with adult representatives of your pastoral team and/or worship team to see who would like to learn from your students.
- **SAY:** Your challenge this week is to find a way to share what you've learned about historical context and Jesus' ministry on the Sabbath with the members of our pastoral/worship team. You can do that in whatever way you like. You can create a video, a skit, a poster, a computer presentation, or plan an activity to do together. You need to work as a group to make your plan.

GET TO WORK

- After the students have decided how they want to share their findings, they can use the remaining time together to execute their plan. Make appropriate materials such as posterboard, video cameras, and a computer available for their use. If possible, have the students present to their adult pupils during the last ten to fifteen minutes of your time together. If not, schedule another time to present.

BLESSING

- Invite your students to bless each other as they prepare to go out and share what they've learned. Students may anoint one another's hands with an unused tube of lip balm while saying a simple blessing, such as "God be with you as you share the good news."

Notes

Where? Geography

Why does this matter?

When it snows in Texas, everything closes. When it snows in Massachusetts, it's business as usual. When urbanites in New York talk about the weather, they're making small talk. When farmers in Kansas talk about the weather, they're talking about work. When it's windy in North Carolina, it makes for a nice breeze. When it's windy in Oklahoma, it could be dangerous. Everyone's life is shaped, to varying degrees, by their geography.

Modern city dwelling folks are less likely to be aware of the effects of geography, but people in Bible time were sharply aware of their relationship with the land. For them, geography was a life-and-death subject, not a boring class. People in Bible times didn't have maps as we know them, scaled guides of the local landscape. Without a bird's-eye view, the biblical authors' only way of knowing their geography was to explore it and occasionally get lost in it.

Long trips were inherently dangerous, because the prospect of becoming lost without access to food or water was real. Food preservation was difficult, so travelers relied almost entirely on the hospitality of strangers to feed and shelter them. For long trips or moves, people traveled in large family groups and brought their livestock with them. Travel was arduous. In short, being away from or without your own plot of arable land made you vulnerable.

Even when the Israelites did settle in Canaan, their survival was not guaranteed. Long droughts like the one in 1 Kings 17–18 threatened the Israelites' survival. No wonder the Israelites placed such spiritual and religious value on the land as God's promised blessing. The land was life. The poignancy is gone from many modern people's relationship with the land. As a result, we often overlook geography. Imagining the biblical landscape enriches our ability to enter into the biblical narrative. Stories become more textured when we imagine the sensory experience of wandering in the desert or sailing on the Mediterranean. We better understand the urgency of Mary and Joseph's flight to Egypt, or the passion that the magi must have felt to travel all that way. In short, biblical geography reveals a new layer of meaning.

Supplies

- study Bibles (CEB)
- Bible atlas
- compasses (smartphones often come with a compass)
- Student Journals
- small sticky notes
- prewritten orienteering routes
- dry-erase board and marker set
- pens, colored pencils, markers
- presentation supplies such as posterboard, video camera, computer/tablet

Learning Goals

- Spark curiosity about the biblical landscape
- Prompt reflection on the relationship between land and daily life
- Use archaeological research and biblical maps to explore biblical geography

In the Brain of a Tween

You may think you need to have all the answers in order to do an in-depth Bible study for tweens. I've got good news for you: you don't! In fact, your students will probably prefer it if you avoid handing them answers. Instead, let the students take the lead in the investigation. Your job is to ask good questions, encourage their imagination, and intervene as needed to keep the group on track.

Some tweens have relatives who hunt or farm. Others have experience camping and learning wilderness survival skills. Others have next to no experience with the outdoors. Tweens who have spent time in the wild will have more appreciation for the relationship between geography, survival, and culture. Whatever their experience level, all tweens can benefit from exploring biblical geography. Biblical geography can help visual and sensory learners engage with the stories, and shed new light on well-known narratives.

Explore

PLAY TOGETHER—ORIENTEERING

○ Before class, create one or more orienteering routes through your meeting space. Choose a common starting place and mark it with a sticky note on the floor or wall. Use a compass to determine the direction from the starting place to the second point on the route, and count the number of steps between them. Write down these two pieces of information for each step in the route. A sample step might read: 180°—12 steps. Mark each point with a sticky note. Use different colored notes to distinguish between different routes. Place about five points on each route.

○ Divide the students into groups of three to five. Give each group a compass and assign a route.

○ Invite the groups to complete their routes, collecting each sticky note as they go, and return to the starting place when they're done.

○ **ASK:** Have you ever **orienteered** before? Was it easy to follow my instructions? Can you imagine using this method to travel many miles?

○ **SAY:** In biblical times, maps drawn to scale didn't exist. If people wanted to travel long distances, they relied on methods like the one we just used to get from place to place. It was easy to get lost, so they had to know how to survive from the land. Geography was a life-or-death situation in biblical times!

Bible Geography 101

When you hear the word *geography*, what do you think? If you're like most people, you think of maps. But geography is about much more than national borders or navigation.

The geography, or landscape, of your homeland shapes your life in important ways. Your local geography determines the food you eat, the clothes you wear, the type of house you live in, and more.

Now that we live in a globally connected world, we're not completely limited by our geography. We can eat a banana grown in Jamaica, pull on a T-shirt made in Cambodia, and ride in a car made in Japan—all before we arrive at school. Even so, it's likely that if you live on the Maine coast, seafood is a regular part of your diet; and if you live in Alaska, you own a heavy coat; and if you live in Oklahoma, you know where to take shelter during a tornado.

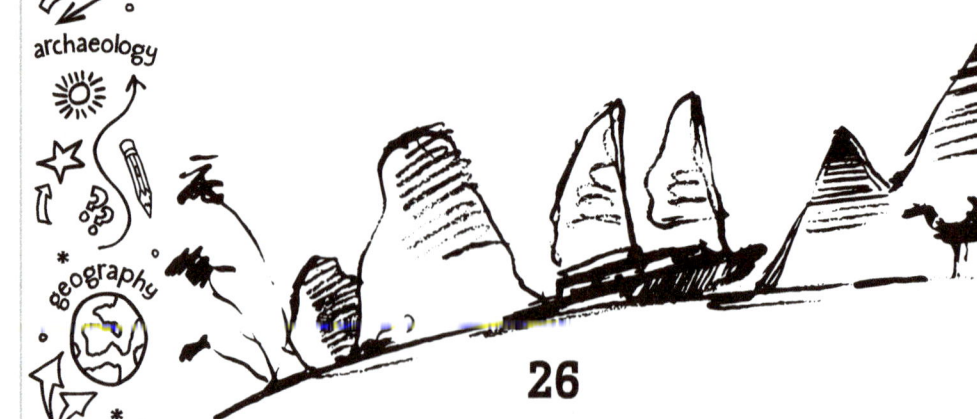

EXPLORE

○ Play Together—Orienteering
○ Explore the Theme
○ Try It Out—Your Geo-graph

STUDY

○ Connect It—Biblical Landscape
○ Read a Text—Exodus 16:1-21
○ Use Some Tools—Study Bible, Bible Atlas

Your Geo-graph

Okay, so you know that your local geography affects your life. But HOW does your local geography affect your specific life? Answer the questions below to create your very own personalized Geo-graph. Circle all that apply.

I live near:

mountains	rivers	
fields	lakes	volcanoes
the ocean	forests	the jungle

The weather where I live is usually:

sunny humid rainy windy

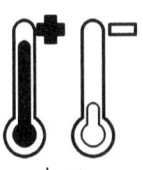  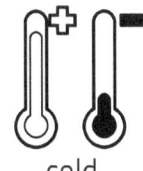 

hot dry cold snowy

We have to watch out for:

| blizzards | hurricanes | landslides |
| tornadoes | flash floods | volcanic eruptions |

EXPLORE THE THEME

- Invite students to take turns reading pages 26-27 of their Student Journals out loud.
- **ASK:** What parts of your life are the most affected by your local geography?

TRY IT OUT— YOUR GEO-GRAPH

- Invite students to pair up and complete the Your Geo-graph activity on pages 28-29 of their Student Journals.
- Invite each pair of students to share their responses.
- **ASK:** How might your **geo-graph** be similar or different from an ancient Israelite's geo-graph?

REFLECT

- Journal
- Discuss
- So, What?

SHARE

- Make a Plan
- Get to Work
- Blessing

Study

CONNECT IT—BIBLICAL LANDSCAPE

○ Invite the students to turn to pages 30-31 of their Student Journals and read about the biblical landscape.

○ **ASK:** How familiar were you with the biblical landscape before now? What's one thing you learned that you didn't know before?

READ A TEXT—EXODUS 16:1-21

○ Invite the students to find Exodus 16:1-21 in their Bibles and take turns reading the passage out loud. If you aren't sure all your students are familiar with the story of the Exodus, give them a brief recap of the events that occurred before this passage.

○ **ASK:** How do you think geography might affect the experience the Israelites had wandering in the wilderness? What would you like to find out about the geography of their journey?

○ Write the students' questions on a dry-erase board. If the students don't readily come up with questions, help them along with suggestions. Possibilities include: What food is available in the desert? Is manna real? How far is it from Egypt to Canaan? Where is the Reed Sea? How hot was the desert they were in?

Biblical Landscape

Most of the stories in the Bible take place in Israel, a land that was small, but packed with diversity.

The land of ancient Israel contained high mountains (Mount Hermon is 9,000 feet!) as well as the Dead Sea, which is the lowest point on the earth's surface. Parts of Israel were dry and desert-like, and other parts were humid and close to the Mediterranean Sea.

USE SOME TOOLS

○ Invite the students to explore their questions using a study Bible and Bible atlas.

○ **ASK:** What information have you gathered? How does this information shed light on our story?

Journal

Now that you know more about the wilderness the Israelites wandered in, it's time to interpret the story. What does the wilderness symbolize to you? Have you ever been in a spiritual wilderness?

Reflect

JOURNAL

○ Invite the students to spend some time in individual reflection, responding to the prompt on page 32 of their Student Journals.

DISCUSS

○ Invite the students to share their responses as they feel comfortable.

○ **ASK:** How does learning more about the literal wilderness help you understand the symbolic wilderness? What does this story teach us about being in a wilderness and relying on God?

SO, WHAT?

○ **ASK:** What does geography have to do with biblical interpretation? What difference does it make? How would you summarize our discussion today in one sentence?

○ **SAY:** Much of the information we have about the geography of the biblical world comes from archaeology.

Share

MAKE A PLAN

- Before class, check in with the person in charge of your children's ministry to identify a children's Sunday school class that your students could share their findings with.
- **SAY:** Your challenge this week is to find a way to share the story of the Israelites' wandering in the wilderness with some of the younger kids. You can do that in whatever way you like. You can create a video, a skit, a poster, or plan an activity to do together. You need to work as a group to make your plan.

GET TO WORK

- After the students have decided how they want to share their findings, they can use the remaining time together to execute their plan. Make appropriate materials such as posterboard, video cameras, and a computer available for their use. If possible, have the students present to their pupils during the last ten to fifteen minutes of your time together. If not, schedule another time to present.

BLESSING

- Invite your students to bless each other as they prepare to go out and share what they've learned. Students may anoint one another's hands with an unused tube of lip balm while saying a simple blessing, such as "God be with you as you share the good news."

Notes

Why? Interpretation

Why does this matter?

Interpretation is the work of the human brain. Our brains are constantly at work interpreting the world around us and all forms of communication therein. Imagine two people hiking in the woods. They each see a large, brown form ahead. The first person interprets the shape as a fallen tree trunk, and hardly reacts. The second person interprets the shape as a bear, and quickly becomes frightened. Each person's interpretation of the shape happened in fractions of a second, unconsciously.

When we read the Bible, our brains process the text through its already existing frameworks. These might be called our "interpretive lenses" because they filter information before it even arrives at our conscious brain, just as eyeglass lenses filter visual images before our brain processes them. It's our job to identify our interpretive lenses and be aware of them as we read the text. Only then will we be able to understand how we can read the same text as another person and arrive at opposing interpretations.

In addition to interpretive lenses, there are interpretive layers we must acknowledge. The biblical text arrives in our hands (or on our screens) at the end of a centuries-long process of interpretation. Between us and the original audiences of the Bible, there are translators, canonizers, scribes and copyists, editors, authors, and oral storytellers. Each of these represent a separate interpretive layer; each person who wrote, edited, copied, canonized, and translated the text made interpretive decisions.

Through all these layers and lenses, we read the Bible and make meaning from it. The task is, at times, daunting. This is why belief in the guidance of the Holy Spirit in hearing and understanding God's word is so essential. It's also why reading the Bible in community is crucial to faithful interpretation. We read our holy Scriptures in community so that we might hear the interpretation of people in different life situations. Only then can all the facets of God's word come to life. You and your students have an important part in the sacred, communal adventure of interpreting the Bible.

Supplies

- study Bibles (CEB)
- various Bible translations
- Bible commentary
- Bible dictionary (CEB)
- Bible concordance
- Student Journals
- Class Pack
- cardstock
- colored cellophane (red, green, and blue); scissors; clear tape
- pens, colored pencils, markers
- dry-erase board and marker set
- presentation supplies such as posterboard, video camera, computer/tablet

Learning Goals

- Create awareness of interpretive lenses and layers
- Spark curiosity about our own and others' interpretive lenses
- Use a concordance and various translations to compare meanings

In the Brain of a Tween

You may think you need to have all the answers in order to do an in-depth Bible study for tweens. I've got good news for you: you don't! In fact, your students will probably prefer it if you avoid handing them answers. Instead, let the students take the lead in the investigation. Your job is to ask good questions, encourage their imagination, and intervene as needed to keep the group on track.

Many tweens are old enough to have noticed that people's life experiences affect how they see the world. Even an example as simple as whether one sees the glass half-full or half-empty will resonate with their lived experience. That lived experience may not naturally translate to the Bible, especially if they've been taught that the Bible has one meaning or interpretation. Introducing the Bible's "interpretive layers" and the long history of differing interpretations might give your students the freedom to add their own voice to the conversation.

Explore

PLAY TOGETHER—COLOR FILTERING GLASSES

- Before class, print out the Eyeglass Frames (Class Pack—p. 3). If possible photocopy the eyeglass frames onto cardstock. Print out the Filtered Lens Test Cards (Class Pack— p. 4) and cut them apart.

- Give each student a pair of frames to cut out. While the students are working, cut the colored cellophane into rectangles about the size of the frames.

- Allow each student to select three cellophane rectangles *of the same color* for his or her lenses. Have the students trim the lenses down to fit their frames, then carefully tape the cellophane in place. (**NOTE:** Clear tape will cancel the effect of the cellophane lenses, so be sure students don't tape over the section they'll look through.)

- Have the students experiment with the Filtered Lens Test Cards (Class Pack—p. 4) by comparing how many circles students wearing different colored lenses can see.

EXPLORE THE THEME

- Invite students to take turns reading pages 34-35 of their Student Journals out loud.

- **ASK:** Which interpretive layer seems the most important to you? Why?

Layers and Lenses

There are **layers to interpretation.** There are also lenses. Lenses and layers. Layers and lenses. How do you keep track of all those *L*'s? Here's a breakdown of the lenses and layers of Bible interpretation:

Layers

Between the original author and the modern reader, the Bible passes through many hands. By the time the Bible gets to you, it's already gone through several layers of interpretation, which have influenced the meaning.

1. **The Translators**—The Bible was originally written in Hebrew, Greek, and occasionally other languages. You can read the Bible in English thanks to the work of translators. If you've ever learned a foreign language, you know that translation can be tricky. Words and phrases in one language don't translate neatly into another. Take the English phrase "I ran into him at the store." If you translated that word-by-word into another language, the reader might imagine someone literally sprinting into another person. In order to get the true meaning across, the translator needs to figure out how to convey the idea of coincidentally meeting someone at the store. Translators have to decide the best way to communicate all kinds of words and phrases in another language, and that's interpretation.

2. **The Canonizers**—How did the Bible become the Bible? Why were some stories, letters, and gospels preserved while others faded into obscurity? The answer lies with the canonizers. The canonizers are the people who decided which books were important enough to be in the *canon* or the Christian Bible, and what order they should go in. Most of the canonizers were Christian leaders during the second to fourth centuries.

EXPLORE

- Play Together—Color Filtering Glasses
- Explore the Theme
- Try It Out—Name Your Lenses

STUDY

- Connect It—God's Image
- Read a Text—Genesis 1:1-31
- Use Some Tools—Study Bible, Bible Dictionary, Concordance, Commentary

Name Your Lenses

What are you like? How do you see the world? What's your unique perspective? Use the following open-ended questions to begin naming some of your lenses!

Do you speak the same language at home and at school?

Have you ever felt singled out because of race or ethnicity?

Do you feel like there are some activities you should or shouldn't do because of your gender?

Are you tall, short, or in-between?

Do you have a disability that affects how you move, learn, or interact with others?

TRY IT OUT—NAME YOUR LENSES

- Invite students to pair up and complete the Name Your Lenses activity on pages 36-37 of their Student Journals. Remind the students that they won't be sharing their responses with anyone else.

- **ASK:** On a scale of one to ten, how much do you think your life experience affects how you read the Bible? Why?

REFLECT
- Journal
- Discuss
- So, What?

SHARE
- Make a Plan
- Get to Work
- Blessing

TIP
- Display the Bible Safety Checklist (Class Pack—p. 5) during this session. Refer to it as you guide the students through **Read a Text—Genesis 1:1-31** on the following page.

Study

CONNECT IT—GOD'S IMAGE

○ Invite the students to pair up and complete the God's Image activity on pages 38-39 of their Student Journals. Invite students to share their interpretation of the statement: "God created humanity in God's own image" (Genesis 1:27).

○ ASK: How many different interpretations did we come up with just in our group? Why do you think the poet made such an open statement, rather than spelling out what the words meant? Do you think there are better interpretations than others?

READ A TEXT—GENESIS 1:1-31

○ SAY: Let's back up and read what comes before this section.

○ Invite the students to take turns reading Genesis 1:1-31 out loud.

○ SAY: We're going to do a bit of research to help us understand what it means to be created in God's image. Let's start with the basic questions we've already learned to ask: Who wrote this? What genre is this? When was this written? And where?

○ Write the questions on the dry-erase board.

○ ASK: What other questions do you have that might help us interpret verse 27?

○ Write any additional questions on the dry-erase board.

God's Image

Did you know that one of the most debated parts of the Bible is in the very first chapter? Genesis 1 is a poem about Creation. The poet says that God created humanity in "God's own image." For centuries, Jews and Christians have tried to understand what that means. What's your interpretation?

Read Verse 27, and what comes after it, in Genesis 1:27-31.

> ²⁷God created humanity in God's own image,
>
> in the divine image God created them,
>
> male and female God created them.
>
> ²⁸God blessed them and said to them, "Be fertile and multiply; fill the earth and master it. Take charge of the fish of the sea, the birds in the sky, and everything crawling on the ground." ²⁹Then God said, "I now give to you all the plants on the earth that yield seeds and all the trees whose fruit produces its seeds within it. These will be your food. ³⁰To all wildlife, to all the birds in the sky, and to everything crawling on the ground—to everything that breathes—I give all the green grasses for food." And that's what happened. ³¹God saw everything he had made: it was supremely good. There was evening and there was morning: the sixth day.

38

USE SOME TOOLS

○ Divide the students into small groups. Have each group use a different tool to investigate the passage, choosing between a study Bible, a commentary, a Bible dictionary, and a concordance.

○ If students don't understand how a concordance works, give them a quick lesson.

○ ASK: What information have you gathered? How does this information shed light on our story?

Journal

Now that you've investigated other people's interpretation of the meaning of "God's image," what do YOU think? What does it mean to be created in God's image? How does this passage affect how you see yourself? How you see others?

40

Reflect

JOURNAL
- Invite the students to spend some time in individual reflection, responding to the prompt on page 40 of their Student Journals.

DISCUSS
- Invite the students to share their responses as they feel comfortable.
- ASK: Do you think your study of this passage will have an effect on how you live your life? Why or why not?

SO, WHAT?
- ASK: What do lenses and layers have to do with biblical interpretation? What difference do they make? How would you summarize our discussion today in one sentence?

- SAY: We have lots of tools to help us investigate the meaning of biblical passages. In the end, it's up to us to determine, through prayer and reflection, what the Bible means to our lives today.

Share

MAKE A PLAN

- Before class, talk with your pastor to find out the best way for the students to share what they've learned with the congregation. It may be possible for the students to perform a skit or deliver the sermon in worship one week; they might create a display for the fellowship hall; they might film a video for the website. Find out what options are available and present them to the students.

- **SAY:** Your challenge this week is to find a way to share what you've learned about being created in God's image with the congregation. Here are some ideas I've looked into. [Insert options here.] You need to work as a group to make your plan.

GET TO WORK

- After the students have decided how they want to share their findings, they can use the remaining time together to execute their plan. Make appropriate materials such as posterboard, video cameras, and a computer available for their use. Schedule any necessary follow up for the students to complete their plan.

BLESSING

- Invite your students to bless each other as they prepare to go out and share what they've learned. Students may anoint one another's hands with an unused tube of lip balm while saying a simple blessing, such as "God be with you as you share the good news."

Notes

How? Read Closely

Why does this matter?

When we read the Bible today, we have turnable pages or scrollable screens. We can have Bible verses delivered to our email in-boxes. We can study the Bible with apps that show us multiple translations at once. Our Bible ease-of-use rating is off the charts. It's hard for tweens, who have always lived in a computerized world, to imagine the effort that went into creating these ancient texts. It's even hard for adults, who have always lived in a world with printing presses, to imagine the arduous task of copying manuscripts by hand.

In our biblical ancestors' economy of words, each word held much more value than it does now. The people who wrote, edited, and copied the biblical text didn't take a single word for granted. Every word was carefully chosen by authors, copied by scribes, and memorized by illiterate people of faith. When we practice reading the Bible closely, we honor the careful work of our ancestors.

We also strengthen our "faith muscles" by paying attention. Simone Weil, a French Catholic theologian, argues that prayer is the highest form of paying attention, of opening oneself to God. Any lesser form of paying attention, such as studying the Bible, only strengthens one's ability to pay attention in prayer.

Many of us read the Bible and begin drawing conclusions about the meaning before we even finish reading. This tendency to interpret on autopilot impedes the process of paying close attention to a text. Why would we need to read it carefully if we already know what it means?

Christians who read the Bible carefully are often surprised by what they find. For example, in nearly every nativity set there are three magi figures. If most Christians were asked why, they'd respond that the Bible says three magi visited Jesus. But the Bible doesn't say there were three magi. Much of what we assume the Bible says comes from our cultural Christian traditions. This is a small example. In other instances, a failure to read carefully might yield a more drastic difference in interpretation. The goal of this session is to slow down and read carefully by paying attention to the four possible meanings, or "senses," that Jewish and Christian interpreters have historically looked for in the biblical text.

Supplies

- study Bibles (CEB)
- Bible dictionary (CEB)
- Bible concordance
- Student Journals
- Class Pack
- pens, colored pencils, markers
- white paper
- dry-erase board and marker set
- presentation supplies such as posterboard, video camera, computer/tablet

Learning Goals

- Cultivate appreciation for our ancestors' preservation of the biblical text
- Practice reading carefully
- Discover the four senses of Scripture and practice interpreting them

In the Brain of a Tween

You may think you need to have all the answers in order to do an in-depth Bible study for tweens. I've got good news for you: you don't! In fact, your students will probably prefer it if you avoid handing them answers. Instead, let the students take the lead in the investigation. Your job is to ask good questions, encourage their imagination, and intervene as needed to keep the group on track.

Interpreting the Bible according to four senses, or meanings, is an ancient practice. Today, people of faith often present only two options for interpreting Scripture: literally, or figuratively. Strict literalists often give the impression that there is only one "right" interpretation of Scripture; strictly figurative readers often dilute the bold claims of Scripture to the point of truisms. Neither approach helps tweens apply the Scriptures to their lives. The four senses of Scripture is an interpretive framework that allows tweens to take the Scriptures seriously, while not limiting them to their literal sense. Often Scriptures that are difficult to apply in their literal sense are rich in symbolic, allegorical, or comparative meanings.

Explore

PLAY TOGETHER—DRAW A DOLLAR

○ Make white paper and colored pencils available. Give students five minutes to recreate, in the most detail possible, an accurate drawing or verbal description of a dollar bill. Students should represent both sides of the bill. Don't allow the students to look at a bill for reference.

○ After the time is up, compare the students' drawings or verbal descriptions with a real dollar bill. Discuss what they were able to depict accurately, what they drew or described inaccurately, and what they left out entirely.

○ **SAY:** You have seen a dollar bill countless times before this. Yet, just because something is very familiar to us, that doesn't mean we pay close attention to it. The Bible is the same way. We may have heard Bible stories dozens of times, but have never read them carefully.

EXPLORE THE THEME

○ Invite students to take turns reading pages 42-43 of their Student Journals out loud.

○ **ASK:** What do you think of these four ways of reading the Bible? Which one seems the easiest? Which one seems the hardest? Do you think it's possible for these ways of reading the Bible to contradict one another?

Four Meanings, One Text

How many different ways can you read one passage of the Bible? Well, since the Middle Ages, some Jewish and Christian Bible interpreters have believed there are at least four ways. Their lists didn't match up perfectly, but each tradition listed four unique ways to interpret Scripture. Here's a mash-up of the two lists:

1. The literal, or plain meaning.

Christian interpreters called this the *literal sense*. Rabbis called this the *peshat*, from the Hebrew word for "surface." This way of reading takes the text at face value.

2. The comparative meaning.

The comparative meaning is the meaning passages take on when read in connection with other parts of the Bible. Christian interpreters called this the *allegorical* or *typological sense*. Rabbis called this the *derash*, from the Hebrew

42

EXPLORE

○ Play Together—Draw a Dollar
○ Explore the Theme
○ Try It Out—Interpret a Fairy Tale

STUDY

○ Connect It—Captain Obvious
○ Read a Text—Genesis 22:1-19
○ Use Some Tools—Study Bible, Bible Dictionary, Concordance

Interpret a Fairy Tale

Let's try out the first three forms of interpretation with a common story—"Little Red Riding Hood." If it's been a while since you've heard the story, here's a recap:

Little Red Riding Hood is a little girl named after the fancy, red cloak she wears. One day, her mother sends her to visit her granny with a basket of food. Her mother warns her to stay on the path through the forest.

A Big Bad Wolf is also in the forest. He spies Red and follows her for a while. He approaches her and asks her where she's going. Red tells the Wolf she's visiting her granny. The Wolf suggests that she pick some flowers for Granny. While Red is picking flowers, the Wolf goes ahead of her and eats her granny!

The Wolf puts on Granny's clothes and waits for Red to arrive. Red notices immediately how different Granny looks. She comments, "My, what big eyes you have!" The Wolf responds, "The better to see you with, my dear." Red says, "My, what big ears you have!" The Wolf responds, "The better to hear you with, my dear." Red exclaims, "My, what big teeth you have!" The Wolf growls, "The better to eat you with!" then proceeds to eat Red as well. Fortunately, a hunter drops by, cuts open the Big Bad Wolf, and rescues Little Red Riding Hood and her granny.

44

TRY IT OUT—INTERPRET A FAIRY TALE

- ○ Invite students to pair up and complete the Interpret a Fairy Tale activity on pages 44-45 of their Student Journals.

- ○ Invite each pair to share their responses to questions 2 and 3 with the group.

- ○ **ASK:** Do you think interpreting a fairy tale is easier or harder than interpreting the Bible? Why?

REFLECT

○ Journal

○ Discuss

○ So, What?

SHARE

○ Make a Plan

○ Get to Work

○ Blessing

Learning to Study the Bible
Leader Guide: Session 6

Study

CONNECT IT—CAPTAIN OBVIOUS

- Display the Four Senses of Scripture Poster (Class Pack—p. 6) for the students to refer to as they do this activity.
- Invite the students to pair up and complete the Captain Obvious activity on pages 46-47 of their Student Journals.

READ A TEXT—GENESIS 22:1-19

- Invite students to take turns reading Genesis 22:1-19 out loud, then share their responses to the questions in the Captain Obvious activity. Write them on the dry-erase board under the heading: "Literal."
- **SAY:** Now let's tackle the "Comparative" and "Symbolic" meanings of the story.

USE SOME TOOLS

- Divide the students into two groups.
- Have one group investigate the comparative meaning of the story by looking up the related passages listed in a study Bible (these are usually found in the margin). They might also look up interesting words in the concordance to see how they are used elsewhere.
- Have the other group investigate the symbolic meaning of the story by reading the notes in a study Bible and looking up potential symbols in a Bible dictionary.
- Have each group write their findings on the dry-erase board under the appropriate headings.
- **ASK:** Which of these meanings makes the most sense to you? Why do you think Jewish and Christian interpreters came up with these four ways of looking at a story?

Captain Obvious

When you're interpreting the literal sense of a biblical passage, you can feel like Captain Obvious. You're just saying the same thing in your own words. You're stating the obvious.

That's okay! That's an important part of Bible study. Because the truth is, most of the time the *literal meaning* of the text IS obvious. But sometimes it isn't. It's always good to check for a basic level of understanding by restating the main points of the passage in your own words. If that exercise isn't easy, you may need to do some more research to understand the literal sense of the text.

It's your turn to be Captain Obvious. Check out the story in Genesis 22:1-19. Then answer these basic questions:

Journal

Now that you've explored the first three senses of the story, it's time to explore the "secret sense." What does this story in Genesis 22:1-19 mean to you? What is God saying to you through this story? What special meaning does it hold for you?

Reflect

JOURNAL

- Invite the students to spend some time in individual reflection, responding to the prompt on page 48 of their Student Journals.

DISCUSS

- Invite the students to share their responses as they feel comfortable.
- **ASK:** Do you think every passage in the Bible has a "secret sense"? Why or why not?

SO, WHAT?

- **ASK:** Why should we read the Bible carefully? Why do we need to pay attention to the different kinds of meanings in the Bible? How would you summarize our discussion today in one sentence?

Share

MAKE A PLAN

- **SAY:** Your challenge this week is to find a way to share what you've learned about the story of Abraham nearly sacrificing Isaac with your family. You can do that in whatever way you like. You can create a video, a skit, a poster, or plan an activity to do together. You can work individually or in small groups to make your plan.

GET TO WORK

- After the students have decided how they want to share their findings, they can use the remaining time together to execute their plan. Make appropriate materials such as posterboard, video cameras, and a computer available for their use.

BLESSING

- Invite your students to bless each other as they prepare to go out and share what they've learned. Students may anoint one another's hands with an unused tube of lip balm while saying a simple blessing, such as "God be with you as you share the good news."

Notes

How? Reread

Why does this matter?

The first six lessons of this study teach students how to analyze the Bible by drawing on the findings of historical criticism, literary analysis, biblical archaeology, and more. Those methods of study are invaluable to the modern reader. They illuminate the biblical text by clarifying its origins, de-centering our modern point of view, and drawing us into the strange and exciting world of the original authors and audiences. By studying our ancestors' encounters with God, we open ourselves to our own encounters with God.

Now it's time to turn our focus away from the world of the authors and toward our own responses as readers. Reader-response criticism is a method of interpretation that centers the readers' experience of a text and role in making meaning. Reader-response criticism balances a tendency to focus entirely on the original authors of the Bible, ignoring the vital role of the reader.

If the biblical text is the "living word of God," then its meaning cannot stagnate in ancient Israel. It must also be capable of making new meaning as new people of faith experience the text. Both the historical context and the readers' context are important in Biblical interpretation. This belief is not a new-fangled theological response to changing times. It is an ancient belief that is fundamental to Christian biblical interpretation. As early as the New Testament, Christians re-interpreted the Hebrew Scriptures in light of their experience of the resurrected Christ.

By the third century, a Christian theologian named Origen taught a method of prayerfully reading the Scriptures through the lens of Christ, as a way to draw closer to God. He called this method "divine reading," and throughout the centuries, Christian monks have distilled the general method into four steps: *lectio* (read), *meditatio* (meditate), *oratio* (pray), and *contemplatio* (contemplate). This basic method has been adapted into various steps for different audiences. It typically involves reading the same Scripture several times in a meditative fashion. This lesson engages the students in a creative, age-appropriate form of divine reading.

Supplies

- Bibles (CEB)
- Class Pack
- Student Journals
- pens, colored pencils, markers, and a permanent marker
- various art supplies such as oil pastels, watercolors, colorful paper, modeling clay, and so forth
- candle and matches
- meditation beads (or pony beads, yarn, and adult scissors)
- presentation supplies such as posterboard, video camera, computer/tablet
- device for playing music (optional)

Learning Goals

- Create awareness of our own role in making meaning
- Prompt reflection on the nature of Scripture as the "living word of God"
- Practice the ancient tradition of divine reading

In the Brain of a Tween

You may think you need to have all the answers in order to do an in-depth Bible study for tweens. I've got good news for you: you don't! In fact, your students will probably prefer it if you avoid handing them answers. Instead, let the students take the lead in the investigation. Your job is to ask good questions, encourage their imagination, and intervene as needed to keep the group on track.

Many tweens are more comfortable with a scholastic investigation of Scripture than a spiritual encounter with it. Tweens may have never engaged in spiritual practices in a group, and their initial reaction may be discomfort and giggling. That's okay! Divine reading is a practice, not an achievement. God can still speak to uncomfortable tweens. Try to trust the process and avoid intervening in uncomfortable silences. Lighting a candle or playing meditative music can help set a worshipful tone during your practice.

Explore

PLAY TOGETHER—AD LIB

○ Before class, print out the Ad Lib Story (Class Pack—p. 8).

○ Have the students supply the nouns, adjectives, verbs, and other words asked for in the Ad Lib Story. Use a permanent marker to fill in the blanks.

○ Have a student read the ad lib to the class.

○ **SAY:** Today we're focusing on what we bring to biblical interpretation. We don't fill in words like we did here, but we do bring our unique perspective to every passage we interpret. God speaks to each of us through the Bible, so our life experiences are an important part of interpretation.

EXPLORE THE THEME

○ Invite students to take turns reading pages 50-51 of their Student Journals out loud.

○ **ASK:** Do you see yourself in the biblical story? Where? Do you see the Bible as your book, or your story? Why or why not?

Divine Reading

Over the past few weeks, you've learned a ton about how the Bible was created. You've explored who wrote it, what kinds of writings are in it, when and where it was created, and why all of that matters. You've learned about layers and lenses of interpretation, and four senses of Scripture. Your Bible knowledge is expanding rapidly!

Now it's time to shift the focus. Let's talk about YOU. Yes, you. The Bible isn't just about the people who created it. If it were, why would we still be reading it after all these years? The Bible is also about you. It's your sacred story, and it's your life that is affected by how you relate to the Bible.

EXPLORE

○ Play Together—Ad Lib

○ Explore the Theme

○ Try It Out—Finish the Picture

STUDY

○ Connect It—DIY Divine Reading

○ Divinely Read a Text—Psalm 139:1-6

○ Use A Tool—Meditation Beads

Finish the Picture

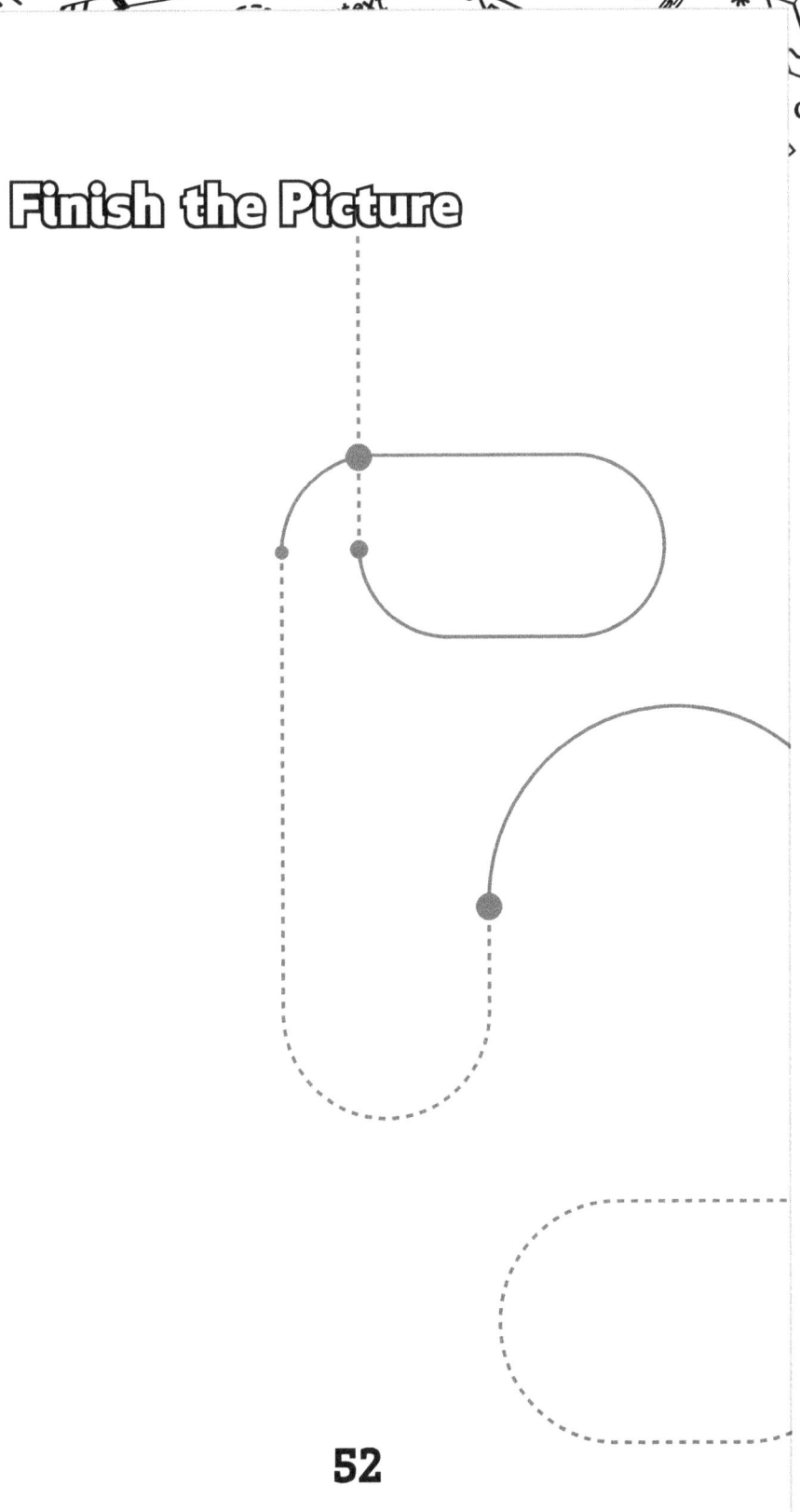

52

TRY IT OUT—FINISH THE PICTURE

- Invite students to complete the Finish the Picture activity on pages 52-53 of their Student Journals.
- Invite the students to share their completed pictures as they are comfortable.
- **ASK:** What influenced your artistic decisions in this process? Why did all these pictures turn out differently, even though you started with the same image?

REFLECT
- Journal
- Discuss
- So, What?

SHARE
- Make a Plan
- Get to Work
- Blessing

Learning to Study the Bible
Leader Guide: Session 7

Study

CONNECT IT—DIY DIVINE READING

- Invite the students to read about the method of divine reading on pages 54-55 of their Student Journals.
- Invite the students to choose the artistic materials they would like to use during their meditation, prayer, and contemplation of the passage.

DIVINELY READ A TEXT— PSALM 139:1-6

- Display Lectio Divina Steps (Class Pack—p. 7) for the students to refer to as they do this activity.
- Invite the students to find Psalm 139:1-6 in their Bibles. Solicit four volunteers to read, one for each step below.
- Light a candle before you begin. Turn on quiet instrumental music if you like. Invite the first student to read the passage.
- **ASK:** What part of the passage "shimmered" or stuck out to you?
- Invite the second student to read the passage out loud. Allow a few minutes of silence for the students to use their art supplies to meditate on the passage.
- Invite the third student to read the passage out loud. Allow a few minutes of silence. Invite the students to pray silently about whatever the passage brings up for them as they continue working with the art materials.

48 Learning to Study the Bible
Leader Guide: Session 7

DIY Divine Reading

1. Read

This step is pretty straightforward. Read the passage carefully. Notice any words or phrases that "shimmer" or stick out in your mind.

2. Meditate

In this step, let your brain get creative with the passage. As you or someone else reads the passage again, draw or paint whatever images come to you, rewrite a verse, or doodle as you go over the passage in your mind.

54

USE A TOOL

- Give each student a set of meditation beads. (You can easily make meditation beads by stringing yarn with eight to ten pony beads and knotting each end.)
- **SAY:** During this last reading, we will be contemplating the Scripture, or listening for God to speak to us through the passage. Listening in silence can be a difficult task for busy minds.

Permission is granted to duplicate this page for local church use only. © 2018 Abingdon Press.

deepbluekids.com/learningtostudy

Reflect

JOURNAL
- Invite the students to spend some time in individual reflection, responding to the prompt on page 56 of their Student Journals.

DISCUSS
- Invite the students to share their responses as they feel comfortable.
- **ASK:** How do you listen to God in your daily life?

SO, WHAT?
- **ASK:** What does divine reading have to do with biblical interpretation? Where are you in the biblical story? How would you summarize our discussion today in one sentence?

Meditation beads give our hands something to do as we listen quietly.
- Invite the fourth student to read the passage. Allow the students about two minutes of silent contemplation using their meditation beads. To end the time, **SAY:** Amen.
- **ASK:** What was the easiest part of that reading for you? What was difficult for you? What insights did you gain from that way of reading Scripture?

Share

MAKE A PLAN

- **SAY:** Your challenge this week is to find a way to share what you've learned about divine reading with your family. You can do that in whatever way you like. You can create a video, a skit, a poster, or plan an activity to do together. You can work individually or in small groups to make your plan.

GET TO WORK

- After the students have decided how they want to share their findings, they can use the remaining time together to execute their plan. Make appropriate materials such as posterboard, video cameras, and a computer available for their use.

BLESSING

- Invite your students to bless each other as they prepare to go out and share what they've learned. Students may anoint one another's hands with an unused tube of lip balm while saying a simple blessing, such as "God be with you as you share the good news."

Notes

How? Read Together

Why does this matter?

We think of the Bible as one book, because we have the luxury of reading it in bound copies. Even those who study the Bible, and recognize it as a collection of disparate texts, created over centuries, tend to speak of the "biblical narrative," or "overarching story of the text." Those may be helpful shorthand ways to refer to our inherited faith, but they don't do justice to the diversity of voices within the biblical canon.

Cohesive narratives are created by one author, or by authors working in concert. The biblical authors didn't have the luxury of checking in with one another to discuss where the enterprise was headed. Some biblical authors clearly had access to other texts that would eventually become part of the Bible. But the collection of texts that make up the canon are piecemeal perspectives on the story of Israel and the Jesus movement that emerged from it. If those who canonized the Scriptures had truly preferred a single, cohesive narrative, they could have omitted books, edited others, and crafted a much smoother story. Instead, they carefully preserved a library of diverse, and at times contradictory, perspectives. Rather than giving us an epic saga, they gave us an epic conversation.

We who have inherited bound copies of the "book" known as the Holy Bible have been given an immeasurable gift. We have a bird's eye view of the sacred stories of our spiritual ancestors. We can see the connections, the comparisons, and the inter-canonical conversations that those who created the text never could have seen. We can weave multiple threads into one larger conversation. But it's important to remember the integrity of each thread on its own. In our eagerness to unearth the "one story" of the Bible, we may find ourselves cutting away threads that seem unnecessary or stubbornly unwilling to be woven into our narrative. We can make the mistake of Martin Luther, who was so convinced that the story of the Bible was "justification by faith alone," he concluded that the Book of James had to go. Rather than glossing over the Bible's dissonant voices, our ancestors invite us to wrestle with them, enter the conversation, and find our own place in the story of faith.

Supplies

- study Bibles (CEB)
- Bible commentary
- Bible dictionary and concordance
- Student Journals
- pens, colored pencils, markers
- device that can access YouTube
- dry-erase board and marker set
- presentation supplies such as posterboard, video camera, computer/tablet

Learning Goals

- Create awareness of the diversity of voices within the canon
- Inspire students to enter into the centuries-long biblical conversation
- Practice reading the Bible inter-canonically

In the Brain of a Tween

You may think you need to have all the answers in order to do an in-depth Bible study for tweens. I've got good news for you: you don't! In fact, your students will probably prefer it if you avoid handing them answers. Instead, let the students take the lead in the investigation. Your job is to ask good questions, encourage their imagination, and intervene as needed to keep the group on track.

Tweens are at a transitional moment in their faith. Many are preparing for confirmation or graduation from the children's ministry. They are asked to take ownership of their faith as they begin individuating from their family unit. For many tweens, this is a pressure-filled time. They don't feel invited into a conversation; they feel pressured to agree to beliefs they don't entirely understand. Helping tweens view the Bible as an epic conversation between our spiritual ancestors reframes the conversation. Rather than being asked to agree with an already formed conclusion, tweens are invited to join in an epic conversation between people of faith and God. That sounds like a much better deal to most of these curious, questioning kids.

Explore

PLAY TOGETHER—MAKE A SCENE

○ Invite your students to stand in a circle. Choose one person to begin forming the scene. That person runs into the center of the circle, forms a shape, and announces what they are, as in, "I'm a tree!" or "I'm a chair!"

○ The next person in the circle must immediately run into the center and form a shape that adds to the scene. For example, "I'm the sun shining on the tree!" or "I'm a cat napping in the chair."

○ Continue this way until the entire group has contributed to the scene. Then choose another student to begin a scene. Encourage the students to see how quickly they can form a scene.

○ Continue playing as long as time and interest allow.

○ **SAY:** In that game, we created a scene by building on what the people before us did. Many of the biblical authors built on what had been written before them. The Bible is like a big conversation. There are all kinds of connections between books. We're going to explore some of those today.

EXPLORE THE THEME

○ Invite students to take turns reading pages 58-59 of their Student Journals out loud.

○ **ASK:** Why do you think Marcion's teachings were so appealing to some?

Canon Connections

Back in the days of the early church, being called a "Marcionite" was a big insult. Marcionites followed a guy named Marcion, who argued that the teachings of Jesus were completely incompatible with the God of the Old Testament. Thus, he believed that the God of the Old Testament could not be Jesus' father.

Marcion's teachings were rejected by the early church. Even though church leaders recognized some differences between the Hebrew Scriptures and the Gospels, they also saw deep connections. They believed that the teachings of Jesus built upon the teachings in the Hebrew Scriptures. Rather than throwing out the Old Testament, early church leaders reinterpreted it in light of what Jesus taught.

It can be tempting to view the Bible as one epic story, with a plot that perfectly progresses with each book. Marcion thought that's what the Bible should be, so he threw out the parts that didn't match his idea of the biblical story. But the Bible isn't one big story. The Bible is more like one big conversation. There are diverse perspectives, and they don't always easily fit together. But the many voices of the Bible help us understand the many angles of truth

58

EXPLORE

○ Play Together—Make a Scene

○ Explore the Theme

○ Try It Out—Musical Conversations

STUDY

○ Connect It—The Lord Is My Shepherd

○ Read a Text—John 10:1-16

○ Use Some Tools—Study Bible, Bible Dictionary, Concordance

52 Learning to Study the Bible Leader Guide: Session 8

Musical Conversations

Inter-textual conversations don't just happen in the Bible. They happen all the time in popular music. Sometimes, musicians use tunes or lyrical phrases from songs that came before them to create new songs. This is called *sampling*. Other times, musicians combine two songs into one new song. This is called a *mash-up*. In a mash-up, two songs that were unrelated before have a "conversation" and take on new meaning.

Consider the popular mash-up of "Amazing Grace," the famous hymn written by John Newton in 1779, and "Peaceful, Easy Feeling," released by the Eagles in 1972. Even though these songs were written almost 200 years apart, they mash-up perfectly. Take a moment to listen to the mash-up. (You can easily find a video of it on *youtube.com*.)

60

TRY IT OUT—MUSICAL CONVERSATIONS

○ Invite students to pair up and complete the Musical Conversations reading and questions on pages 60-61 of their Student Journals.

○ Play a version of the Peaceful, Easy Feeling/Amazing Grace mash-up. You can easily find a version by searching YouTube or most music streaming apps.

○ Invite each pair to share their thoughts and responses as they are comfortable.

○ **ASK:** Can you think of any other songs that sample other tunes? What do you think the practice of sampling tunes has to do with the Bible?

REFLECT
○ Journal
○ Discuss
○ So, What?

SHARE
○ Make a Plan
○ Get to Work
○ Blessing

Study

CONNECT IT—THE LORD IS MY SHEPHERD

- Invite the students to pair up and complete The Lord Is My Shepherd activity on pages 62-63 of their Student Journals.

- **ASK:** What connections did you see between the Ezekiel passage and the Psalm?

READ A TEXT— JOHN 10:1-16

- Have the students find John 10:1-16 in their Bibles and take turns reading the passage out loud.

- **ASK:** What connections do you see between this passage, the Ezekiel passage, and the Psalm?

- **SAY:** Let's use our Bible study tools to make a portrait of the different people in these passages.

USE SOME TOOLS

- Divide the students into groups to investigate the different characters: the Good Shepherd, the ordinary shepherds, the thieves, the sheep. Have each group gather information on their assigned group using the study Bibles, commentary, Bible dictionary, and concordance.

- Have each group report their findings. Write them on a dry-erase board.

The Lord Is My Shepherd

Psalm 23 is what you might call a classic. Chances are, you've heard it before. You may even have memorized it when you were younger. Take a moment to refresh your memory:

¹The Lord is my shepherd.
  I lack nothing.
²He lets me rest in grassy meadows;
  he leads me to restful waters;
    ³he keeps me alive.
He guides me in proper paths
  for the sake of his good name.

⁴Even when I walk through the darkest valley,
  I fear no danger because you are with me.
Your rod and your staff—
  they protect me.

⁵You set a table for me
  right in front of my enemies.
You bathe my head in oil;
  my cup is so full it spills over!
⁶Yes, goodness and faithful love
  will pursue me all the days of my life,
  and I will live in the Lord's house
  as long as I live.

62

- **ASK:** How does our knowledge of the Ezekiel passage and the Psalm help us understand what Jesus is saying in John 10:1-16?

Journal

Does thinking of the Bible as a conversation rather than a story change how you interact with it? Do you see yourself as a part of the biblical conversation? Why or why not?

_____

_____

_____

_____

_____

_____

_____

_____

_____

_____

_____

Reflect

JOURNAL

- Invite the students to spend some time in individual reflection, responding to the prompt on page 64 of their Student Journals.

DISCUSS

- Invite the students to share their responses as they feel comfortable.
- **ASK:** How are you in conversation with the Bible? How does the Bible connect to your life?

SO, WHAT?

- **ASK:** Why are the connections between biblical passages important? What difference do they make? How would you summarize our discussion today in one sentence?

Share

MAKE A PLAN

- **SAY:** Your challenge this week is to find a way to share what you've learned about the biblical canon with your family. You can do that in whatever way you like. You can create a video, a skit, a poster, or plan an activity to do together. You can work individually or in small groups to make your plan.

GET TO WORK

- After the students have decided how they want to share their findings, they can use the remaining time together to execute their plan. Make appropriate materials such as posterboard, video cameras, and a computer available for their use.

BLESSING

- Invite your students to bless each other as they prepare to go out and share what they've learned. Students may anoint one another's hands with an unused tube of lip balm while saying a simple blessing, such as "God be with you as you share the good news."

Notes

www.ingramcontent.com/pod-product-compliance
Lightning Source LLC
LaVergne TN
LVHW061317060426
835507LV00019B/2192